# Looking Through My Eyes

## Bill Wagner

ISBN: 978-1-959700-29-6

# Dedication

To my brothers and sister for their love and for the experiences they allowed me to share. I love you. God bless you all.

# Contents

# Preface

One of the fears I face in writing a book is if I want to relive all that I went through. Do I want to remember all the comments made? The "You're stupid," "You should meet him, he's just like you." There's a lot this old boy from southwest Virginia went through that he tried to keep to himself. Talking about it may do him good.

As I look back on my life, I can see one thing that has always been there. God has watched over me. I always liked church and missed it when I wasn't there. It was the fun of being there with friends. Listening to the music and I did like to listen to the preachers. Getting together after church with Aunt Beulah and singing to the top of our lungs— well, it was just a great time.

Many friends and family have gone on now. It's hard to remember all the good times we had. The ones that are still here try to share some of those times. I hope that in this book, no one is offended. I am trying to tell my story through 'my' eyes. God has blessed me through these years. He has given me peace in my old age. Some wisdom and good health. A loving, godly wife to keep me close to Him.

# Chapter One

"You should meet him. He's just like you." Words that never seem to go away. Growing up in the Brickyard, the dreams we had as children were few. We never really knew what was ahead of us. Some of us didn't think we would live as long as we have. In this part of the state, we were considered poor. I never saw it this way. We always had plenty to eat, clothes to wear, and a roof over our head. By today's standards, we were dirt poor. When I talked about where I was from, people would think that we were in the Appalachian part of the state. We were part of the Appalachian Mountains but not Appalachia. That was coal mining country. They were living a pretty rough life. They didn't have a lot of what I got to enjoy. I think the media and television made people get the wrong idea of where I was from.

We used to play in the creek. Fish in the creek. Some kids even set the creek on fire on Halloween. The worst thing about the creek was that everyone's sewer ran into the creek. We didn't care. We still did what we did. Today I tell people that if they think anything is wrong with me, maybe it was what was in the creek we played in.

We never had to worry about people bothering us while I was growing up. We would play outside all day. Go up into the woods. Stay for hours. Swing on grape vines. Get into rock fights. Play baseball, football, or whatever in the cow pasture. If we got hungry, we would go to a friend's house. Their parents always gave us something to drink and eat. It was like one big family. Always looking out for one another. On Sunday, you would see about all of us kids in church. The parents didn't come that often, except when we would have special programs for them to see. I figured they needed some parenting time alone. As we grew older, some of them got driver's licenses and had their own car. That didn't happen to us. I was in my 20s and married before i ever got a car. I didn't have a driver's license until I was in Vietnam. That was an experience that I'll tell later.

Graduating High School, getting a job, and moving out was a lot of our plans. I had wanted to graduate, get married, have a good job, have kids, and have a nice home. I never thought about a car much. I always seemed to get a ride. Always walked where I went if I couldn't get a ride. Didn't live too far from work starting out. I didn't make a lot of money early on, but it was enough for rent, clothes, utilities. That's all that seemed to matter. If the wife and I went out, it was usually with friends and they had a car.

Life changed a lot after I got a car. It seemed there was always an added expense. Tags, insurance, repairs. But we felt like we needed one. Work was good and I was making good money after a few years.

Early in my marriage, things didn't go too well. We had only been married a couple of months and my wife started having doubts. She thought she loved someone else. It was her best friend's brother. Being immature, I said, "Why don't you go and spend the weekend with her and find out?" Well, she went and spent the weekend. When she came home, she still didn't know how she felt. It wasn't much longer that she said she was pregnant. I asked if it was mine. She said she didn't know. Devastated, I decided to go into the military. Vietnam was going on and frankly, I figured I would go there and get killed. The child would be taken care of and I would be out of everyone's life. It wasn't God's plan, but at the time, it was mine.

## Chapter Two

Everyone I knew that was married stayed married. That's the way it was where I grew up. There were no divorced couples. Everyone married for life. My sister had married and it was rough to start with, but they got through it.

I had gotten married on June 6, 1970. Two hours later, I graduated from High School. That was strange, I guess, to get married and graduate on the same day within hours. We had gone to the preacher's house that afternoon. I can't remember who all was there. A lot of time has passed. You would think that you could remember the details of your first wedding.

We had worked at the same business. A local fast-food restaurant. I had worked there before I was married. My mother- in-law, wife's girlfriend, and my best friend at the time worked there. One night, we had gotten busy. My wife went outside and was talking to a girlfriend. She came in and my boss came in behind her. He was mad. He started chewing us out. The next day, he met us at the beginning of our shift. He fired my wife, mother-in-law, wife's best friend, then gave me the option of staying. I said, "No way."

She didn't get a job after that and I found work at a local furniture factory. We moved so it would be closer to work. I would walk down the railroad tracks to work. It wasn't long that we found out that our landlord was slipping into our trailer, checking it out. She found some cat food. She didn't allow cats in her trailers. We didn't have one, but my wife was feeding a stray. We had to move. Back in the other direction we went. Having to find a ride to work after moving into an apartment next to the first place we lived.

It wasn't long after that we moved again. Closer to where I grew up, actually beside my grandmother.

## Chapter Three

A few days before I was supposed to go to the Induction Center for the Army, I burnt my foot. I was helping my friend and his friends kill hogs. I was lifting a bucket of hot water out a barrel over the fire when the bucket tipped and I spilled the hot water on my foot. I had boots on but it got wet enough to redden my foot. When I got to the Induction Center, they said that my foot would have to heal up before I could be examined. I went home until after Christmas.

The twenty-seventh of December 1970, I went to the Induction Center in Roanoke, Virginia. After the examination, I was put on a bus headed to Fort Campbell, Kentucky. Didn't get to go home and say goodbye. It was the next day before I could call home. We rode a bus to Bristol, Tennessee, where we got on a plane to Nashville. Strange because Roanoke had their own airport. Anyway, at three a.m. in the morning, I arrived at Fort Campbell. Fort Campbell, Kentucky, Home of the 101st Airborne. I actually stayed in their barracks because they had been deployed to Vietnam.

There was a couple weeks of testing and shots. That was my first experience with an air gun that was used to give shots. It was weird. Shooting medicine across the room to make sure the guns were working. As I stepped up for the shot, the technician would say, "Don't move, you don't want to get sliced." Some guys did get sliced because they moved. One night in the barracks next to ours, the MPs busted a guy for showing a porn movie. It was the movie *Deep Throat*. Odd that I would remember that detail. Anyway, we were moved out in a couple days to start our basic training. January and February in Kentucky isn't always the best time to start training. Snow, cold, was the norm. Always wearing extra layers when we went to the rifle range. I don't think I was ever warm.

The platoon that did the best during the week, whether it was on the range, at the barracks, or in the classroom always got to lead the company in marching to the range. Needless to say, we were a platoon of misfits. Some regular Army guys, reservists, and national guard made up our platoon. We changed platoon leaders a couple of times while there.

Our Drill Instructor wasn't too hard but hard enough. We respected him. One of our platoon members helped him with a correspondence course he was taking. He was hard but he was respected. When our training was near the end, we had to take a PT test. We had only 8 or ten who didn't pass the first time, where there were nearly half of the other platoons had to retake it over. Our DI was excited. He had some bragging rights. It must have been all the times we were last in marching. Graduation came soon and we all got orders for our AIT, advanced infantry training. Some of the guys went to Fort Jackson or Fort Stewart for infantry and parachute training. I got sent to Fort Sam Houston, Texas, for training.

Fort Sam Houston was divided into two parts. Up the hill and down the hill. Strange because the land was so flat. I grew up in the hills of Southwest Virginia and there weren't any hills in Texas. Down in the lower part of the fort was training for combat medics. That's where I started. I guess the testing at Fort Campbell determined where I was going and what my job in the Army would be. Two weeks of medic training, then they sent me up the hill. I was assigned to a class to be a Medical Technician.

Ten weeks in the spring in Texas. There's a lot of crazy weather. I saw my first tornado while I was there. We got up high on a building and watched it go down to the south. It's fascinating at a distance. The weather was hot. The hardest thing we did was that we had to march to classes. It was up a little rise, but not bad. We learned how to take blood from one another. How to process and test it. What to look for. We also did that for our own urine and fecal tests. That was so different. Taking blood was the most difficult. We would draw blood from one another. Different body types. Some thick, some thin. It was hard when you couldn't see the vein.

After twelve weeks, we got our orders. Some got to stay stateside, but most went overseas. One guy from New York was sent to Africa. He was a short person and we made fun of him. Most of the guys got orders for Vietnam. Our commander called the MPs, Military Police, and told them that we were going to be partying pretty hard. The MPs came around but kept their distance.

There was an Airborne soldier in our group. He made some Airborne mash. Pure grain alcohol and fruit juice. Everyone got pretty drunk. Even one guy who was going to Fort Riley, Kansas. He had never drank alcohol before and did he ever get wasted. He was so sick the next few days. One guy from northern Virginia had some pot. I had never been around anyone that smoked pot. I was getting pretty wasted and I asked him for a smoke. I took a draw off the pipe he had and my head cleared up. My body was still drunk but my mind was clear. We went downtown San Antonio to Krispy Kreme donuts. We had the munchies.

In a couple of days, we all departed. Some of us got to go home for ten to fourteen days. It worked out good for me. I got to see my son born. It was wonderful. The joy of being a father, even if there was doubt that he was mine. Now, heading off to war. What will it be like? Will it be like the movies? The war programs on television? You know, Combat. Mash. The Dirty Dozen. The Green Berets. I have no idea what to expect. There's a fear but also a peace. It will be what it will be.

## Chapter Four

Where was God? For about eight years, I hadn't spent much time in a relationship with the Father. I had basically walked away from Him. I had stopped praying. Stopped reading my Bible. Convinced I was going to Hell and that there was no chance for redemption. It wasn't that God wasn't there, I just wouldn't let Him in. I was doing so much wrong. Walking away from what I had been taught growing up. Sinful and unclean. Filthy rags.

I got on a plane at Tri-Cities Airport in Tennessee. Flew to Atlanta where there was a layover. I met some guys that were doing the same as me. Heading to Vietnam. We flew from there to Seattle, Washington. More GIs were there, readying for Nam. We boarded a Flying Tiger Airlines commercial jet. The airlines initials were FTA. Our meaning stood for F*&k The Army. Wasn't very nice but our whole outlook on life was about to change.

We landed in Anchorage, Alaska, to refuel for our trip across the Pacific Ocean. A long flight. We wondered if the plane would make the flight. When it had landed in Alaska, the wings seem to flop a lot. Fortunately, we made it. Landing in Cam Rahn Bay, South Vietnam.

It was about midafternoon when we landed. There was shelling on a hillside near the airbase. For hours the Army would lob shells into the hillside, pause, send in the helicopters. If they got shot at, the shelling would start all over again. This went on the whole time I was there.

It was too early for supper, so some of us went to the NCO club to get a beer. While I was there, I met a friend from my hometown who was on his way home. We sat and talked for a long time. Making fun of our meeting, his leaving, and my entering. I was getting pretty lit while we were there, so I went to lay down before supper. When I awoke, it was too late for supper, so I proceeded to go to the NCO club for a meal. It was closed. My friend and his buddies had gotten drunk and got into a fight. They shut the place down. I never saw him again, even after I came home.

I proceeded from there to Long Binh, then to Bien Hoa. There we got trained in doing our job while in Vietnam. We were the first unit to be sent to drug test the soldiers leaving the country, going on R&R. There was a lot of drug use and it was a valiant effort to stop but it couldn't be. Today, we see some of the results of that addiction. The drug testing was in its early stages and many got through because they knew how to manipulate the system. Soldiers would get a doctor to say that the reason they tested positive was the medicine they were on from an injury in the field. Too often, it worked.

Our unit proceeded to Saigon, now Ho Chi Minh City. Camp Alpha was our destination. Attached to Tan Son Nhut Air base. A lot of traffic there and a lot of mortar attacks from the Viet Cong.

Camp Alpha was a transfer station. People leaving the country came through Camp Alpha. Out the front gate was Saigon, the capital of South Vietnam. It was a place you wouldn't venture into alone. The Ninth Medical Hospital was located there. I would venture there in a few months.

All this area, the air base, Camp Alpha, was on an Air Force Base. We were near the Saigon River, so the Navy was close by. If we needed anything, the Navy or Air Force would have it. We visited them to get the materials to build our rooms. There was just about anything you would want in a small, confined city. We had a library where I would spend many hours trying to stay faithful. Question was, what was I being faithful to? I wasn't divorced yet.

The strangest thing about being in a drug detection unit was that there were more drugs than what you would imagine. I wasn't there long until I was introduced to all kinds of drugs. A couple of the guys were dealing. Their fate would be sealed in time. One day, we were hanging out when these guys pulled out some joints. You know, marijuana cigarettes. I smoked my first joint in Nam. When you get down to the last of the cigarette and you can't hold it, you get tweezers and finish it. The last of it is called a roach. I told them my story about roaches. The ones I talked about were the many legged kind that crawled across your food while you were eating. The kind that exterminators have to come in and spray. I said, "Man, I know about roaches. My mother-in-law had some of the biggest ones in her house." They all cracked up.

## Chapter Five

When a soldier is far from home, it's hard sometimes to be faithful, especially if there is a divorce looming in the future. I spent the first couple of months doing what most new soldiers do. Well, those who are stationed in what is called the rear. But in Vietnam, there was no rear. There was danger everywhere. I stayed on base, doing what all good boys do. I hung out at the library, recording reels of music for the reel-to-reel tape player that I purchased. I miss that music box. I recorded hours on hours of music. Country. 50s rock-n-roll. 60s rock. Music that I would spend hours listening to. Lying in bed, whether it was time to sleep or just take a nap. I wrote home often. That was the hardest part. I missed my family. I would get letters from mom about how the wife was just lying around doing nothing. Letting the baby cry a lot from wet diapers and such. Them having to get up during the night and take care of him because the wife was still asleep. Then the wife moved out.

I would get letters from the wife about how hard it was at my parent's house. How she had to move because she couldn't stand it anymore. She moved in with her parents and it was almost that bad. Mom always asking for more money to help pay the bills, especially the phone bill that her brothers would run up. Her two oldest brothers were in the service. The oldest was in Vietnam and he would call home a lot. The other was in training stateside, making collect calls. The calls I made were supposed to be free from overseas. The only difficulty was the time. There was several hours difference in time from Vietnam to Virginia. Then my sister-in-law would write me and tell me how both families would be so hard on the wife. My wife would tell me that she needed me to come home. I said I couldn't. I'm in a war zone and I just couldn't pack up and leave. I didn't think that the Army would consider it a hardship just because my wife couldn't get along with the families. I stopped writing as much. It was too much for me to handle.

I had some dental issues that I had to get taken care of. In the military, nothing short of an emergency is done until you reach your permanent duty station. Our family didn't do too much for dental hygiene. Maybe it was the area we lived in. Maybe it was the state of the economy. We probably just couldn't afford to go to a dentist. With a family of seven, two adults and five children, it wasn't very possible to have a regular dentist visit. As my parents got older and the kids out of the house, they were able to afford dental work. That mostly in the form of dentures. I think all the kids had some form of dental work, my sister and I had full dentures.

That's what went on with me. I had to wait until I got to my permanent duty station. Vietnam. I saw the dentist on the base and he confirmed that all my teeth were so bad he had to remove them all. The surgery was scheduled and right after Thanksgiving in 1971, I went into the hospital in Saigon, the 9th Medical Hospital. All my teeth were removed. While I was in the recovery room, I found out that the Vietnamese were superstitious about losing teeth. The aid that was checking on me asked me if I had 'fini' all my teeth. I said yes and I never saw her again.

I was put on a ward for recovery. I had an IV and some more antibiotics. Man, was that an eye opener there. There were about 100 guys on the ward with only two nurses, that I saw, per shift. They had their hands full. There were guys all around me that had been wounded in combat. I felt so ashamed. Here I was in a hospital for dental surgery and there were guys across from me that lost arms and legs. Who didn't have the help to get them out of their beds to go to the restroom or go take a shower. They had to do it themselves. My heart ached. I vowed I would never say anything bad about a stateside hospital no matter what. We never realize how blessed we are.

The nurses were so busy that they had let my IV run out. Blood was going back up the tube. My arm started to ache, but I wouldn't complain. When one of the nurses finally saw it, she said that she was so sorry. I said for her not to worry, there were more important needs than mine. She just smiled. After about 24 hours and drinking a ton of liquids, I was able to go back to my unit. That would be another adventure.

When you get around a bunch of military men with perverted minds, a lot of remarks were made. They won't be printed here. The funniest thing they did was they always asked me to smile. It makes me smile to remember.

Christmas Day 1971, I received my new teeth. They felt awkward. Eating was a new experience. My mouth felt way too big. After a few days, it got easier. I can't remember if it was right after Christmas or maybe New Year's Day when me and my buddy would venture to the bar to celebrate. I got plastered. A long story made short, my friend Dave from Minnesota, said, "Pops, what can I do for you?" Pops is what they called me because I was the youngest one of the group with a child. I spit my teeth out in my hand and said, "Can you put these in some water?" I laugh just remembering that. I got up the next morning and went to the john to clean them. On the way back, I dropped the lower plate. Tingle, tingle, tingle was all I heard. It had broken in two. I didn't wear the upper that day and went to the dentist. I was scolded for not wearing the upper plate. They used some super glue and put them back together. They were still together when I got them replaced 20 years later. It had been an eventful last six weeks of the year.

## Chapter Six

Conway Twitty would put out a song in 1975 called, *Linda On My Mind*. My dad would sing it a lot in front of my wife. It was and wasn't funny. Early in January of 1972, I had gone to the bar That's how they made their money. Guys buying drinks for them. They would sit with the guy as long as he bought her drinks. The drink was a green tea. I bought one drink and said I can't buy more because I hadn't brought much money. She said, "Okay." We talked a while then moved on. We eyed each other the rest of the night. Our relationship would progress to a higher level. One I should not have gone to but I did.

I started going there more often. Putting to rest the problems at home I couldn't solve. She had put me in this position, now it was no looking back. The unit got some new guys in. One was a guy from Montana. He was in the Navy and the same classification as me, but his training was more intense. He once delivered a baby in an elevator. I think his name was Stan. That's all I remember except that we started hanging out together. He made friends with one of the other girls at the bar. We all started hanging out together. When the girls were not working, we would meet them downtown. Nothing special. We would go out to eat a couple times. Went to the movies. Mostly we went to their homes. I met Linda's mother one time. Linda's lifestyle and that of her mother were a lot different. I could see from what kind of life Linda was living was not how she was raised. Her mother had the traditional black silk outfit. Her teeth were dark from her diet but not rotten. She was very humble and she bowed when we were introduced.

My company commander did not approve of my relationship. He was a good man. Time plays tricks on one's mind and I cannot remember his name, but that he was from Virginia Beach. One day his name will come to me. He has since passed away. He said, "Remember that you are married and you have a child. A family at home." I said, "That is all gone." I reminded him of the situation at home and he still said I shouldn't do what I am doing. That girl just wants to get to the United States and then she will leave you. Like a normal dumb GI, I said no. The affair went on until I left. I told Linda that when I got home, I would get a divorce and send for her. That never happened.

I flew out of Tan Son Nhat Airport. Watching the drug dogs sniff out everyone's baggage. It was hot. May 1972 and it hasn't been long since the monsoon season had finished. Now it was getting hot and dry.

Our flight went to Hawaii. We didn't get much time off on the layover to look around. I just walked around the airport. The weather was beautiful. The scenery was spectacular. I pondered the chance I had to re-enlist. Fifteen thousand dollars tax free, with my choice of duty station. I had said I was going home. Things I had to do. I needed to see the mountains of Southwest Virginia.

We landed in San Francisco in the wee hours of the morning and I got transferred to another plane. I wasn't processing out here, but going to St Louis, Fort Leonard Wood. That's where all the Army records were stored and also the training area for the Army Corp of Engineers, Military Police, and Chemical training. I was there less than twenty-four hours and I was out of the Army. Boarded a plane for Tri-Cities Airport in Bristol, Tennessee. I think somewhere near middle Tennessee, the right engine of the plane caught fire. We had to land near Nashville. I had been in a war zone and now there was fear of dying on a plane heading home.

The person at the airport said that we would go the rest of the way by limousine. Wow! Wouldn't that be so cool. Pull into Bristol in a limo. Well, that didn't happen. I think it was a ten-person van that pulled up. Bummer. It was in the middle of the night and we were going up I-40. The driver didn't let off the gas. At one time, I looked at the speedometer and it was at 100. I hope he doesn't hit anything.

We got in about five in the morning. My family was all there to meet me. My wife and son. What a shock. My dad said that he was looking for a limo, then he saw me getting out of the van. We laughed. Yeah, I thought it was going to be different too.

## Chapter Seven

Home. My mind was not on Vietnam much anymore. The family had questions. My wife had questions. My son was adorable. It was a lot to get used to after all the time in the military. I went and got my old job back and everything returned to normal. Well, almost. My wife still was having trouble with living with my parents, so we moved in with her parents for a while. I looked for a place and got one at the old apartment house where we had lived when we first got married.

I hadn't been back long until things got difficult at work and at home. I worked with a man named Lloyd and he was a ladies' man. Always looking to flirt and connect with any lady that would have him. I had a lady friend there. Her name was Martha and she was a black lady. We would cut up and have fun. One day, I figured it was because I hung around Lloyd so much, the men accused me of having a fling with Martha. I was pissed. I'm a married man with a family. I was trying to make my marriage work. I didn't need that.

It just so happened that one of my neighbors was off work and a few days after the incident at work, he asked me to go job hunting. I had laid out of work so I said okay. We went to the Brick plant in Atkins and applied for a job. I didn't know that my brother, the one next to me in age, was already working there. He came by the house that night and said that the company wanted me to come into work the next day, September 15, 1972. Little did I know that it would be the first day of 42 years. I quit my old job without a notice and went to work at the Brick plant. I was raised at a place called the Brickyard and I was going to work at the Brickyard. Life can be funny at times.

I didn't do much the first day. Worked out in the loading area just doing some clean up until Monday when they assigned me to the Mill Room. That's where the bricks were made. A cleanup man and it was a dirty job.

I still didn't have a vehicle to drive, so I rode with my brother for a while. He would work there for about two more weeks then he left for another job with my dad. He would stay there about 30 years. *A little side note here. This would be a pattern for most of my life. Dad would do things with brother and not include me. Then ask why I wasn't doing anything with my brother. They were close. Brother was always the best athlete, the best hunter, the best fisherman, the one that always did everything right. The one that always did everything mom and dad asked. Only difference, they never told me what was going on until it was done. Our family was never close. We would show up on Thanksgiving and Christmas, but that was about it. Brother wouldn't ask me to go hunting even if I went to his house and asked him if he was going hunting. He would then go with his neighbor. He didn't want me around.* Anyway, with brother being gone, I had to find transportation. Just hired was a guy from Chilhowie, a town just a few miles down the road. He had an old Volkswagen Beetle, straight shift. He would show up in the winter with the windows still froze up because of the heating system. It wouldn't get hot enough to defrost the window. The first few years was an adventure and also some good memories.

Times were still tough. I had joined the Army Reserves in order to make ends meet.

One weekend a month, two weeks out of the year, I would have to meet and go to summer camp. It was tough times. The economy was in a downturn. Gas was rationed. The economy was in a slump. Layoffs were plentiful. There wasn't much choice to do but to ride it out. The whole system seemed to be failing. The Brick plant had shut down for a while, laying off about a hundred people. We had to sign up for unemployment. Their paperwork got messed up and we were back to work before we received our first unemployment check. To top that off, we were getting paid every quarter in the Reserves and that got messed up. It was six months before we got a payday.

Work started to pick up. We were called back and a new plant was being built next door to the old one. More automation and more advancement. All the new jobs had to be posted and I signed for the forklift job and I got it. We would load trucks and railcars with brick to be shipped everywhere. We once sent brick to the Suez Canal. After about 4 years of working there, a sheriff's deputy pulled onto the lot and delivered me divorce papers. I knew that we were getting a divorce, but this seemed all too real. She had charged me with desertion. After work I went to see her. She was gone from the house. Took the kids and everything but my clothes and a mattress with a pillow and a couple of blankets. When I did finally get in touch with her, she said she had to put something down. I said, "I was gone to summer camp with the reserves." Like a fool, I gave in and said okay. Later my landlord would kick me out because he wouldn't allow me to live like this. At least I did get our car back. I had bought it a year earlier with a loan from a guy at work. They called him the bank. He kept money on him all the time.

Well, now a divorce and no place to live. Had to move back in with my parents. My wife had left me for another man. By this time, there were two children in our family. A girl had been born to us a couple years earlier. Like my son, she said that she didn't know if our daughter was mine. Too long a story to tell here and I'm not sure that I want to go there. Anyway, she had the kids, getting most of my money in child-support and then asking for more. A couple years later, our son would come to live with me. My personal life was struggling, but work was improving. I was getting ready to move up.

A job came open in the mining department and I signed for it. Working outside had always been my enjoyment. The only downside was that in the off season, I would be used anywhere and everywhere. I endured and it paid off. In the spring of 1982, one of the supervisors was retiring, leaving an opening in management. The Plant Superintendent had asked me if I wanted to try management. He couldn't guarantee that it would be approved by the home office, but it was a shot. I was also being promoted in the reserves, so everything was looking up. Of course I said yes. My divorce from my first wife had become final. My son was living with me. There was a new woman in my life and I got married. This new lady in my life was once my neighbor. She was eight years younger than me but when she showed me attention, we became quick friends. We started dating and it was getting serious. I was head over hills in love again. It was going great until an old boyfriend came into the picture. This was the first time he showed up. He would again later. We split for a while and I dated another lady. This lady was nice. Worked at the hospital. My son was only staying with me on the days I got visitation, so there was a lot of free time, alone time, empty time. The old boyfriend took off. The girl and I got back together. Still, too much to write here. We moved into a trailer together. My son wanted to live with dad, so he began living with us. We started going to church. It had been years since I had been in church. We were going to the church I was raised in. Guilt started to wear on me and I knew this was not right, living together. Marriage was just around the corner. Back to work. After a little over a year in training, I got the promotion. Downside, we got paid once a month. Man, was that a struggle. Thirty-two years as a supervisor, maintaining several departments. Having to work holidays, weekends, long hours. It was a struggle. Working three lives. The Army Reserves, civilian employment, and family. I think it took a toll. Did I make the same mistakes again? The old boyfriend in the picture? Another divorce on the horizon, but work is going great. The only constant. The only relief.

## Chapter Eight

In 1980, we were living in a decent house, making a decent income. We both have good jobs. My wife has gotten pregnant after a couple of surgeries. An ovary removed and the other cleaned up. It was still a slim chance for her to get pregnant. My oldest son was living with us. His sister was with her mother. In June, my second son was born. We were so excited that this was happening. All was good.

A little over two years later, the plant manager asked if I wanted to train for a supervisor's position. I said yes. It wasn't guaranteed but it was a chance. Some people were jealous. Some were wishing me good luck. A new plant had been built and was doing well. A lot of overtime was there. We had purchased a new house. Work was still good. My ex had taken our son and moved to Texas. That was a turbulent time. She didn't have my permission but she lied and said she had. She was gone a few months, then returned. My oldest son started living with my ex's parents. She then moved away, leaving our son there. There was a lot that happened that my son wasn't living with us. Too much to go into here. I know that later, he had felt that no one wanted him. I feel that he had so much hurt because his parents couldn't get back together. He had told me that before and I said that there was no way and one day, he would understand.

His mother's parents took me to court for more child support. I had been paying it on time, and in some cases, early because they had asked for it. The day I got the court order to appear, I went to their house. His mother was there. A big discussion started about why she couldn't pay the extra. She said if she had to pay, she would take the boy and file herself. That didn't go over well then, and it didn't go well for her in court. Short story, I didn't have to pay. She took the boy and moved away, again. I can so understand how he feels about being bounced around. No one wanting him. That developed into anger and that anger provided him a future that really turned his life around.

In 1983, my training turned into full time salary supervisor. A new chapter in my life. The next year, my second daughter was born. My wife had to go back into the hospital after Christmas for a complete hysterectomy. That was the start of our lives changing again. In 1994, after 17 years of marriage, we divorced. She had stopped taking the hormone medicine she had been on since the hysterectomy. Her attitude changed. She started hanging with her brother and sister. Going to bars like she did before we got together. The old boyfriend showed up and in a couple of months, we split. She moved out and in he moved. The divorce became final later. The day I received the papers, I looked her up. We both cried. Why?

Also in 1994, I retired out of the Army Reserves after twenty years. A lot going on and I wonder how I survived: a divorce, I gave up smoking, my younger son and daughter were living with me, and work got harder. My oldest son had been in college and got drafted into Major League Baseball. That was another story, another chapter through these eyes.

## Chapter Nine

How many people can say they grew up in poverty stricken southwest Virginia, went to Vietnam, was married twice, divorced twice, all before he turned 50? Where was God? Still there. Still faithful.

Early in my second marriage, we were very active in church. Work was still going well and I thought this was where I needed to be. It was a small church. The one I grew up in. We became more active, well, mostly me. I was elected as Sunday School Superintendent. We started having Bible Study, which I led. The Lutheran Church had been using lay people to help fill in for the shortage of pastors. I was doing that also, and I was feeling it. But I don't think God was pleased with me. The more I tried to do what I thought was right, the harder the struggles would be. We had a part time minister and the rest of the time, the lay people would fill in. The church thought that the part time minister should be the one to bring people into the church. There we disagreed. My brother and sister-in-law had the same view

42

as the congregation. Fought that battle for a while then I left. I wasn't living the right life anyway and God knew that. Until I got my heart right, I couldn't lead.

I couldn't have gotten any farther from God than after I left and went through another divorce. Work was manageable. New bosses come and go. Some that made me want to quit. Some that wanted to fire me. But I survived. More responsibility at work. Including the mining and grinding departments, my added duties was go-for, Training supervisor, water runoff manager (which included testing), and filling in when anyone was off. When my son, the second one, was off to college, it was a little harder on my daughter. She would be home alone a lot. She would call me about staying with her friends, which was okay. I knew she was lonely. Today, I don't think that would be safe for a girl home alone. Soon, she would get a job at one of the local fast-food restaurants. It's comforting to know that your kids want to do well and earn some money. They both did pretty good in school, with my daughter doing the best. She got some serious money when she went to college.

For the next several years, it was crazy. Both the kids were in college. Financial stress is saying it mildly. My daughter didn't need much. When she had car trouble, dad showed up. When money was needed for car repairs or such, what dad couldn't do, big brother would help. His MLB career was going great and we are blessed that he could help. The thing about being in his position, too many people needed help. My daughter was doing good, but she met a boy. You know how that goes. The first one was good, moving up in the retail world. He was being transferred because of a promotion and wanted my daughter to go with him. She wouldn't go and they were no more. She met another boy and in a short time, she was married. She got pregnant and dropped out of school. That was what I was afraid of. Meeting a boy and leaving school. She could have done better than what she did, but that's another story. Three kids later, divorced.

Not much has been said about my oldest daughter. She joined the Navy out of high school. Met a guy, got married, got pregnant, and got divorced. Left the Navy or the Navy left her. Not sure on that. She went through a lot. Didn't get to see her much. She met another man, had two kids by him but no marriage. That man ended up with all three kids and mom was traveling the country. Saw her a few times but couldn't keep up with her. She wasn't around much with her kids. One thing I found out was that no matter who was at fault in the divorce, who was never around, mom was still their mother and they would always look out for her.

The next several years were a whirlwind. One relationship after another. Accused of sleeping with a hundred women. I know that wasn't true, but what I did didn't do anything to change everyone's thoughts. That reputation and being the father of an MLB player, I got to know a lot of people. Invited to a lot of events just because of that. Some were good, some were not. I wasn't known too much in high school, so everyone assumed that the ballplayer was the son of my younger brother. He was often referred to as my nephew, even by the people who knew me.

## Chapter Ten

Where was God? Two failed marriages. Two children I lost valuable time with. My youngest two were with me now, but I was spending so much time at work, they basically grew up on their own. Friends, true friends, come in at a time when one needs them the most. My children's friends helped them get through so much. When children see their parents split, where do they turn? Their hearts are broken, confused. Where do they turn? Parents are so mixed up and angry with themselves, consumed with their own emotions. It took me years to start looking at a divorce through their eyes. It is still hard to imagine. Mom and Dad weren't there that much anymore. Only one at a time when they needed them both. When they showed up at the same time, they were hardly ever alone. A new person in their lives. How could this happen?

Their lives were just starting and it was confusing. Who could they trust? Who could they confide in? The grandparents were divided. Playing 20 questions when they were with them. I got so angry at my mom when she was around the kids. She was the same in the first marriage. Asking questions about the kids' mothers when she should be trying to help them get through this tough time. Maybe she just couldn't see it either. Dad didn't seem to care. Kept a lot to himself, but when he spoke, it wasn't anything pleasant. He degraded me every time we spoke about it. He called me stupid. Our lives were so turned upside down.

One of the only constants was the pastor in the first marriage was the pastor in the second. He had baptized all my children. A good friend of the family. I tried to get counseling from him but the first wife was never around. The second wouldn't do it after what I had told him about our relationship. We still remain friends to this day. We have talked about those times and we both agree, my heart and mind were not right enough with God to find a solution. To find peace. I had tried to do too much on my own. I didn't wait for God to work. To lead me in what I needed to do. I didn't trust Him enough. Too impatient. Too uneasy. Wanted a solution right now. Not wanting to let Him work in His time, His way. A lot that I would learn later in life.

And work? Well, it was hard, very hard at times. Going through all these emotions, daily situations, daily demands, and trying to maintain some kind of sanity. There were times that I wanted to just drive and not stop until the car ran out of gas. Leave it beside the road and continue on. I saw a psychiatrist once and they said I was suicidal. I laughed and never went back. Little did they know that I had already thought of it during my first divorce. A few weeks later, I would try it again. But God spoke to me. He said this and I will never forget it, "Someone has to raise the kids." It took a long time, but I trust God with all my heart.

Back to work. I had one boss who told me that he knew what I was going through. That he was going to keep me so busy, work my butt off, that I wouldn't have time to think about my problems. *That's what you think*, was on my mind. If they only knew the times I was away from work, trying to talk to my wife about coming back, I would have been fired many times over. But a special lady who became a great friend.

I often think that I was still employed because I was well liked by the upper management. Then again, it was because they had a celebrity in their midst. My son had worked at one of the plants during the off season early in his career. They used that as an employment ad to get new people. Later, I got them an autographed photo of him. It was still hanging in the office when I was last there. People were still asking for autographs. Asking how's he doing? Where's he at? Have you got any autographed balls or cards for my kid? Will he be in the area anytime soon? Yeah, it was a benefit.

I forgot to mention the Army Reserves. I was getting close to retiring from there. What a whirlwind of a time. Son drafted into the Majors. Going through another divorce. Trying to quit smoking. Teenage kids at home who needed a full-time dad, and I was gone a lot. We had even been to Honduras for two weeks. That was an adventure. It was during the time the Sandinistas were causing so much trouble in Central America. Luckily, we didn't have any problems while we were there doing road construction.

The year I retired from the Army Reserves, Operation Desert Storm was in the making. We were at summer camp and the word came up to start getting us ready. All our records were being reviewed, making sure they were up to date. It was time for me to get out. I was in one war, I didn't want to be in another. Lucky for us, the battle stopped soon. I was getting out. It took a call to my representative to get the retirement letter I needed. March of 1994 was when I left the reserves. Almost 22 years in the military, counting my time in the regular Army and in Vietnam. Another chapter in my life was over.

## Chapter Eleven

With the military service behind me, I was beginning to have some more free time. The kids were doing good in school. Preparing to further their education in college. Work was still hectic. It would be nice to retire now but that was not in the books. The kids were working after school and playing sports. My youngest daughter was in the band and that was such a thrill. Seeing her in that band uniform made me just as proud as seeing her brothers in the football uniforms. I was disappointed when she quit the band in her senior year. I asked why? Her answer. "I just didn't want to anymore." So much for that. No one on the field to watch for a few years.

September 11, 2001. Did this world change for a little while. Everyone got on their knees and prayed. The world was coming to an end. Our land had been attacked from the air. Terrorists had hijacked some planes and used them as bombs to crash into the Twin Towers in New York City, the Pentagon, and a fourth plane crashed in a field in Pennsylvania. Some brave men took the hijackers on and crashed the plane to keep it from taking more lives. It was believed to be headed to Washington, DC.

I was in a mining supervisors' class in neighboring Wytheville, Virginia. We had to get recertified every so often. After the first session, we took a break. The people in the office started talking about what was happening in New York City. We were transfixed for the next several hours. We completed our training but the day was not the same. I called my daughter and my sons to see how they were. I even called an ex-girlfriend to check on her. Called my mom to check on her. The events of the day were broadcasted for hours on about every station.

I was glad that I was out of the service, but I was fearful for the young men that might be called up. Could this possibly lead to another World War? My old unit was put on alert. The only ones who were called up first were those in transportation. Truck drivers. Some were sent to staging areas, some were sent to transport equipment and supplies. Some even went to the combat site. I was more fearful that I would be reactivated.

And work. Well, it never seemed to change. It was always there. Doing the same thing, day after day. Several new plant managers over the years. New bosses with new ideas, new agendas. I just kept doing the same jobs. I had hopes that some of my responsibilities would be delegated to the new supervisors that would show up. Ones with less seniority, but in management, seniority doesn't matter. It's up to the plant manager who gets what jobs. Mine never changed. At times, there was more to do.

Empty, lonely nights began to fill my time. After work I would go check on my mother. She had been living alone for a while and I was the only one near who would take the time to check on her. My sister had moved away. The brother next to me had a son who was in a terrible car accident. All his time was spent working and taking care of his son. The next brother was living in North Carolina and didn't have time to come up much. Hunting season and some time to fish was his free time to come up. The youngest brother was tied up with being the Recreation Director, so his days and nights were pretty much filled, plus he had children at home to help take care of. So, my life was down to work, checking on mom, and going home.

I had met some old school friends who wanted to get together. This happened back in the 90s. We would get together and chat, then one of them suggested we take up line dancing. Now that was a place I wouldn't have thought I would go.

## Chapter Twelve

Line dancing. The craze of the 90s. Who would know that line dancing would be my relief, my out, my peace, and my self-destruction for the next few years? Many relationships, all gone by the wayside now, that would lead me to do things I never thought I would ever do. I had even professed it as an abomination a few years earlier. Never say never. I thought I grew up with two left feet. Line dancing would show that early through these years. Trying to get my mind and my feet to cooperate was a challenge. My friends and I would practice this in our homes wanting to master these steps. If you have never tried line dancing, I suggest you do it for a while. It will invigorate your mind and body. Make you feel young or make you realize how old you are. There was a group of senior citizens who called themselves the Geritol Teenagers. These people could dance and were willing to help you learn. They taught us to line dance to bluegrass music, rock and roll, hip-hop, just about everything but rap. To watch these people dance, it gave me hope of what I would be like when I got old. I fell in love with line dancing. We even were on television a time or two. There was a television station who had this program, Line Dance, that would let you come and record some shows. That was a thrill later on.

There were a lot of women there. A few that were single, a few married, a few with their husbands, boyfriends, and children. It was a time for family and a time for betrayal. Women who were looking for a good time. Some wanting a new life. A chance to leave the life they felt they were stuck in. That's the 'never say never.' Temptation for a single man looking for some company during the lonely nights. I made several friends and I got involved with one lady who wanted a reason to leave her husband. Well, maybe she had the reason, just had to take the first step. Looking for someone to help with that first step. I was the one but not the one that was meant to be. When you go down that dark road, it's hard to find light. The only light was that she got me back in church. I would stay in that church for 25 years. Still so far away from God, but I feel He was holding on to me no matter how far I strayed.

That relationship lasted a few years after her divorce. She wanted to get married. I didn't. My kids didn't want me to, especially my youngest. She had more wisdom than I had. My kids wanted me to be happy. That was a fleeting thought. Happiness is not found in sin.

For the next several years, it was one relationship after another. Women I had met at line dancing. Women I had met on the internet. Mom said that I shouldn't do that. You don't know what kind of women they are. I told her that they don't know what kind of man I was. If mom had known some of the things I had done, she would have put me over her knee. Women in other states. Married women locally. I never knew how easy it was to find them. Married twice and saw the one side, now I was living the other.

How could God love someone like me? Going to church and doing all I was doing. I saw more of that than one would think. Church going women who were still in the world. Looking for something— that elusive dream. Me, wanting to find that good church going woman who I could settle down with and draw closer to God. The good church going women were not the one God had intended for me. The one who could fulfill my dreams, my hopes, my plans. Again, it wasn't God's plan.

Some that I started dating quit the things I was drawn to. Quit playing the piano. Quit attending church all together. What had I done or was it me? What caused these women to change? One had other problems that I found out after I had fallen for her. Loved her a lot. Found that I wasn't the only one she was using. She had an addiction that meant more than any love she could want. She had a love earlier and was betrayed. I don't think she ever got over that and then she had an accident. Got hooked on the medication that was to help her. She found something more powerful than what the doctors would prescribe. That addiction would cause me to think I could help her leave it. I didn't realize how deep it was and how unprepared I was. It took a lot of time and pain in my life to realize that. I had prayed and prayed for wisdom. One day it came. One day the Lord gave me that wisdom to say goodbye. He never let go of me. He made a way even when I didn't want a way.

## Chapter Thirteen

Walking around the dirt storage building at work one day, I lifted my hands and sang out, "I will praise you in the storm." That's a line from a song by Casting Crowns. I was in a relationship, but I wasn't happy. I knew God wanted more from me, of me, but where was it? I had been listening to a lot of contemporary Christian music: Casting Crowns and Mercy Me and I felt a calling to come home. The home I started crying out to was not this world. Not this home.

So much was seemingly crashing down on me. My finances were in a mess. Collection agencies calling me, and they started calling work. I was afraid for the secretary to take a message because of who would be calling me. I couldn't afford to lose my job, but I was struggling to keep it. Financially, that is.

Work was still going okay. Seems like things change, but then it doesn't. The bosses come and go, but the work, the work life, still seems the same. I was amazed that I still had a job, but no one knew what I was going through and no one cared. As long as I showed up for work, that's all that mattered.

I would sit down and think of where I am, where I have been, and where I am going. The 'where I am going' was the uncertainty. There were nights that I couldn't sleep. Get on the computer and go where I shouldn't go. The only company I had was on that screen, not in the arms of someone. I talked to women all over, trying to make a connection for a little while. Knowing that it would never amount to anything and no chance of ever seeing them. There were some I felt close to and confided in. They shared their problems and I shared mine. I can see why people go there. No physical body to see the next day and feel guilty about.

The kids were out of the house. The two youngest were in college. No one knows how quiet a home is until there is no sound of life in it. The emptiness of a home can chill you to the bone. Coming home and nothing there. The sound of your footsteps as they enter the home. Walk across the floors to an empty kitchen. An empty bedroom. What will I do? There wasn't a time when I wouldn't think of what now? Why now? Sometimes, we long for that solitude, that aloneness, but not now. Not today.

I would think of times as a child when there was so much to do in the home filled with laughter. To go outside and see so much to do. Play with my siblings. That was who we played with the most. My brothers. We would get a ballgame up in the yard. If you could see our yard then, you would wonder how we could play ball. That yard was so big then. We played baseball and football. We would have rock fights, BB fights, play Hide and seek. The other half was mom and dad's. A line to hang clothes on. A garden to plant and feed us all in the fall and winter. Canning as much as we could to get through the tough times. By today's standards, we were poor, but not in our eyes.

I would remember my dad asking me to go with him up to Mr. Stanbury's to get the horse and wagon. All the tools he would need to plow gardens. That's one of the things I remember about my dad. He could handle a team of horses. He would hook up the team to a plow and we would plow the garden. I would watch him work and just sat in awe of what he could do. I can close my eyes and see me behind him in the wagon while he was driving the horses back home. Later, Dad would have a friend who had a tractor to do what he was doing with horses. I can still see me beside him riding that tractor. Life was so full and simple then.

I didn't know of the struggles mom and dad had while raising five kids. We never knew where the money came from but it was always there. We never went cold, hungry, without clothes, or a warm bed to sleep in. Now, in an empty home, I struggled to keep the lights on. The heat going. The truck running. To keep it together.

I was still going to church on Sundays. Sometimes, Sunday night and Wednesday night. If there was anything going on, I would volunteer. I stayed connected, but that's all it was. Connected. A few years back, when I had started back to church, I got baptized. I had a long discussion with my pastor about that. I had been sprinkled as a child growing up in the Lutheran Church, and felt that I was baptized. After a lot of thought, I realized I wasn't. So, I told the pastor I wanted to be baptized. I told my then girlfriend and my daughter what was going to happen. My daughter said her mom wanted to come. I said I didn't care; this was between me and Jesus. The pastor was amazed about who all was there. The funny thing, the next day, the baptistry was empty, completely drained. When I heard about it, I said that my sins were so plentiful that there wasn't enough water to soak them all up.

Up until now, it all seemed like a dream. A mixture of bad, good, and ugly. Joys, heartaches, emptiness, and fantastic events, that one can only dream about, much less, write about. Growing up in the poor south, unhealthy conditions, crowded home, two marriages, two divorces, four kids. Then the grandchildren started coming. It's a joy to have kids, but then grandkids are so much more. By the time I got married for the last time, I had four kids and ten grandkids. I had so much fun with them while they were little and close. When I had time to go spend with them. But as all things, life got busy. Some kids close, some far away. I was still working. I had hoped for an early retirement, but it didn't work out that way. Dreams of a rich son who would support his dad and I would be out of debt, living on easy street. It didn't work out that way and I don't think it was God's plan for me. I wouldn't bet. There's a lot that had happened between my last divorce in 1994 and now 2008. I had been going to the same church for about ten years. I was in a relationship and it just wasn't going anywhere. I would look around for someone else but then I would look away. That's not where I want to be. When a man feels he is trapped and has no hope, will he just quit or keep searching?

## Chapter Fourteen

A new year, a new hope. I would call out to God. My dad had passed and we didn't have a very good relationship. We had argued New Year's Day. He said I didn't appreciate what my brother and sister were doing. That I didn't want my son, the oldest one. That still haunts me today. I told him that he didn't understand. He only saw one side of the problem. He hadn't looked at mine. Were things getting ready to change? Only God only knows.

The church was still growing. Work was as busy as ever. I was wanting to spend more time at one and not the other. Was God calling? The church was having fundraisers. The church was adding on. I was helping set up the booths. Cheryl came out to see how I was doing. The first time we talked, she said that I seemed to be able to do everything. I said I tried to do what I knew. A few months later, we would get together.

The relationship I was in was just not going anywhere. I didn't want to be there anymore, but I didn't know where to go. So, I just stood still. A few weeks later, she would talk marriage and I said I didn't want to get married. A big argument ensured and I was gone. Things were said that I can't even remember, but it was not going anywhere. I got mad. Quit talking to her. Didn't want to make up. It was over even though she tried.

Cheryl asked me if I was still cutting wood. I had been doing that for several years now and giving it away to those in need. No charge. I told her, "Yes." She asked if I could bring her a load. I said, "Of course." She didn't need it. This is a story I love to tell. She says she didn't know why she asked. I took her a load and asked her out to lunch. We went to Cracker Barrel to eat. A friend of ours from church worked there. She told my ex-girlfriend and I started getting calls again. I finally answered and told her it was over.

Cheryl's husband had gotten injured at work a few years ago. The doctors gave him six months to live. He lived five years. He died in 2008. She stood by him and was faithful. Faithful to him and God. She had been going to church again because one of the caregivers had invited her. We had our first date on a hiking trail in Giles County, Virginia. We would go back there again several times. This was all in 2009. We would start seeing each other almost every day. People would tell her that I had a past. She saw all the flags and fell in love with me anyway. I felt this was where God wanted me to be.

It was opening day of the Major League Baseball season. We made plans to go to Atlanta to watch my son play. In our hotel room, I gave her a ring. I had laid it on the dresser while she was getting ready. She came out and said, "Is this what I think it is?" I said, "Yes."

It was May or June when we went out to meet her family in Colorado. They were very welcoming. A few months later, her mom would pass away. I am so glad that I got to meet her. It's a different world in Colorado. Big sky. Rocky Mountains. We have the Appalachian Mountains here, but they have 'the' mountains there. I recall coming home from training in Texas while I was in the Army. So much different than home. When the plane turned over the mountains and the green hills sprung into view, I started singing a song by John Denver. A little twist to it but I sang, "Almost Heaven, Southwest Virginia."

We had our wedding dinner at McDonald's as we then left for the birthday party. So much was beginning to change. So many bad habits, years of living alone, making my own decisions, was coming to an end.

When a person had been making all the decisions and was not dependent on another opinion, conflict is inevitable. She was doing some work from home and I was still full time. I was trying to keep my head up and make it for a couple more years. I was 59 at the time. I have to be honest, there were times I wondered if I had done the right thing, but I felt God was still pulling at me. Saying, "Trust me." This is where you wanted to be, where He wants me to be. I just couldn't see it. Being retired out of the Army for a while, it was starting to pay benefits. The reserves don't pay retirement until you reach 60. You start getting some pay and you come under the military insurance. Wow! That was a shock when we went to get our military IDs. The lady said this will be the best insurance you will ever have. I had been paying for my own insurance through the company. That was a big financial relief on me. I went the next day and canceled it at work. Cheryl had to test the waters first. She had been paying for her insurance, too. It took her a couple months, but she canceled her insurance.

## Chapter Fifteen

There are some people who think that marriage is a game. That you can just call it quits after a short time, if you don't like where you are. What's crazy is that the state can and will allow a no-fault divorce. No fault. That's not what God had told us. One man + one woman = forever. Til death do us part. Where did it go wrong? Too many new laws and too many lifestyles. Man's heart sure did spring a bad leak when he let adultery, fornication, and sexual immorality rule the land. And the sad thing, I did just about all of them. My mother stayed married to the same man even after he passed away. She lived for twenty years and said this, "I buried one man. I don't want another." She seemed to have an abundant life. That's what we get wrong. The abundant life that Jesus spoke of was one of a life with Him. We can have everything we need and live life to the full. When you give your life to Christ and follow Him, it will be full. He will provide you with all you need. You may want other things, go other places, but if you place your trust in Him, your life will be full. Maybe too full when you allow Christ and the Holy Spirit to lead you. Enter Cheryl. I hadn't realized what life could be like until I joined up with her. Doing things that really matter when Christ, when God, is first. Lay it at the Cross and leave it to Him to fix it. He will take care of it. It was a deep journey to deal with that trust. A trust that is more than you ever thought it could be. A door that was opened that you never want to go back through.

What was I in for? A journey that will end in eternity with the Father, the Son, and the Holy Spirit. I don't know if I can put it into words what this journey will be like. I made one statement to some people. This is my last marriage. She will bury me. I sat back and watched her faith in action. I talked to her about her story. The one from where Richard, her first husband, got injured at work and five years later died. How could you have the faith, the strength, to stand by someone like that knowing that one day, they will die? I am about to learn how.

She had a daily routine where she went to the Lord daily. Me, I would try to read some scripture in the morning. Say a short prayer placed with not much emotion, then head out. Still working, I placed my priorities on my day-to-day life, not my eternity. It was a struggle for a long time. I would let the world get the better of me. I would argue with her, saying she didn't understand. She understood more than I would give her credit for. I was the one who didn't understand. I didn't understand what I had to let go of. When I started letting her be my mentor and me her disciple, it all started taking form.

The saying, "A family that prays together, stays together" is a way of life, not just words. She taught me how to pray. How to let the Holy Spirit into my heart, into my life, and trust in Him. We would have prayer together. Have Bible studies together. Offer other friends to have a Bible study in our home. We would buy books by Max Lucado, Louie Giglio, and Andrew Farley and give them away. We would buy two. Do a study where we took turns reading, then give the book away. We wanted others to experience what we had experienced. It's a good thought, but hard to put into action. Many would take our book but only one would read it. We couldn't get them to realize how close you would become to each other when you listened to their voice. One guy said that he didn't know that his wife could read so well. Funny. But you see where this will lead you.

Cheryl would support me, manage the financial part of it, to let me serve others. We had a wood ministry. We would give loads of wood away, only asking for donations if they had it to give. Other than that, don't worry about it. It wasn't supported financially by the church, but the church would let us store wood there. We even kept some split wood there for people just to drive by and get as they need. One gentleman asked me if the people who were getting it deserved it. Who am I to say that they don't deserve it? God has given me the ability, the desire, to put it out there. It's up to Him to judge their hearts, not me. He knows my heart.

We both loved Contemporary Christian Music. We enjoyed listening to Casting Crowns, Mercy Me, Newsboys, Chris Tomlin, Jeremy Camp, and so on. We would go to concerts with younger friends and dance in the aisles. We would have so much fun. The joy of seeing thousands of younger people, teenagers, raising their hands in praise to the Lord God Almighty. All this was working on me. Growing my faith. Wanting to share the Word with everyone. Share my faith and help someone with theirs.

## Chapter Sixteen

When you sit down and want to write about your life, one sometimes has to sit back and think. There has been a lot going on in my life. Vietnam, heavy equipment operator, supervisor. Divorced twice. Four kids. Twelve grandchildren and two great grandchildren. And that's just my side of the family. Cheryl has three kids and four grandkids. When we got married, she told her kids that Christmas would be a little different. There was a lot that was a little different.

I never liked to hike. Well, only as a kid. I liked to ride my bike and I had done that as much as I could. Ride around my hometown, sometimes out in the country. Cheryl and I would ride on trails. I quit riding on the highway when I wasn't able to outrun the dogs anymore. Cheryl's family didn't play sports, but they rode horses for about 40 years. No baseball, no football, no fishing or hunting. That's what most of my family did. They hiked, rode bikes on trails. Her brother was into dirt bike racing. He did it for years. I think that was what brought him to Colorado.

Cheryl had only played some racquetball and did some swimming. In her first marriage, they had a boat and would go on the lake and water ski. We played in the creek with everyone's sewage running in it. We took swimming lessons but I couldn't do it. Always would have a headache when I got in the water. So, I got to wade real good. Still frightens me today to get in deep water and feel myself begin to float. With a son playing Major League baseball, it was a different experience for her. They never went to a baseball game. One time in Colorado, we took her dad, her brother and his family, along with her son and his family to watch the Rockies play. It was a good experience but her dad got too hot. Her dad was a World War II veteran. He got wounded in France when he stepped on a landmine. He didn't like to talk about it except to me and Cheryl's son, Mike. Mike and I had both been in a war, so I think that he could open up to us. My kids played sports. My grandkids played sports. Then we took up golf. I played recreation league softball and got the chance to play against the King and his Court. Eddie Fenner was such a cool guy. I wish I had gotten to know him when he was in his prime. He was in his 60s when I met him. I lied to just get to pitch against him. I hit him in the leg. It was so funny. That's a memory that I like to talk about. Baseball, football, and softball were the sports we played the most. I had two brothers who also excelled in track. I tried wrestling one time. When the guy grabbed me in the crotch, it was time for me to quit.

Growing up, I was a big Yankees fan. Whitey Ford, Mickey Mantle, Roger Maris— those were my heroes. I would imitate being a good pitcher, a great hitter, fast runner. No one could hit one past me. Playing in a make-believe game with the game on the line. The pitcher or the batter, I enjoyed the thrill. Whether I won or lost, I enjoyed the game and I don't think I ever cried in any game I played. Cry if I got hurt. Cry if I got into a fight and lost, which usually happened. Years later, I got to be in Yankee Stadium with my mom. I was so thrilled and she was so scared. The seats were so close together. The aisles were narrow. Super crowded. I was in paradise. Mom said, "Bill, watch your wallet." I just laughed.

So many experiences that I got to

share with my kids: Spring training, Major League stadiums, meeting some of the players, and on one occasion, a friend I went to high school with. When my son played with the Mets, James Raymond Plummer was there. We went to high school together. When our hometown had a farm club of the Mets, he signed up to work for the team. When the team left, he did too. When I saw him, he was a vice-president in the organization. I have a picture with him in the club house of the Mets. We would get pretty good seats at the stadiums, too. Some were super good like the third row in Atlanta, to behind home plate in others. The biggest thrill was when my youngest son and I would go into the clubhouse and sit with the likes of Craig Biggio, Jeff Bagwell, Lance Berkman, and Mike Hampton. To sit in the dugout with Jim Thome and Charlie Manuel and just soak it all in. Not many get to enjoy that memory.

We have a dream of my son making the Baseball Hall of Fame. He's okay with it if he doesn't make it, but it would be really sweet. Growing up, would we ever dream of being in the big leagues? Not hardly. We played in some great games. Imagined that we were the greatest pitchers in the world. The greatest hitters in the world. Yankee stadium was really our front yard or the cow pasture. Sitting in a major league stadium was nothing we would ever expect.

My dad played in a tri-county league when I was growing up. He was pretty good. The ball field was on top of a hill. I don't know how it was graded out, but just past the infield, the outfield would go up on about a 30-degree angle. It was steep. All the drainage would go down to home plate. The field always drained great. Left field would end at the tree line. If a ball was hit over the tree line, it was down over the hill. All the games were on Sunday afternoon. I remember that all the soft drinks were in an old Coca-Cola cooler filled with dry ice. It was some of the coldest drinks we ever had.

Years later, an uncle of ours took us to a Washington Senators baseball game. We sat in the top seats. The players looked like ants. It was one of the biggest thrills I had as a kid. We had a local farm club called the Marion Mets. I loved going to the games just to chase the foul balls. The announcer would always say, "Ball boy, on the bank!" That was so much fun. Nolan Ryan came through there. He only stayed a week and we all know his history.

I played recreation league baseball. I wasn't very good, probably about average. Didn't get in the game much until the regular catcher got hurt. Then the coach put me in to catch. I had to put a handkerchief in my mitt because the pitchers threw so hard. My hand would always hurt after the game and it was really red. Later, in high school, I became a pitcher. A friend of mine asked me to pitch. He said that I had nothing to lose. I had been cut the year before as I tried out for the outfield. I made the team. Won a trophy my senior year for the lowest ERA, earned run average. My recreation league coach asked me one time, "Why didn't you tell me you could pitch?" I said, "You didn't need a pitcher." Still no dreams of ever playing in the big leagues, much less have a son who would make it. And now, a grandson playing in the minors. What a thrill. I would continue to play some baseball. At one time, I played softball during the week and baseball on the weekend. The best game I had, during my first marriage, was the day she left. The second best game was after my second wife left. I was hitting homeruns in softball and baseball then. Strange how the sports I loved playing helped me through some really tough times.

## Chapter Seventeen

Where was God now? I still believed. I still prayed to Him, but only when I needed Him to help me. Not to forgive me. Not to guide me, but to give me what I wanted. Not what I needed. That's what I got. What I needed. I needed to continue in that downward spiral. To keep struggling because I wouldn't give Him my heart. Years of struggling. Years of praying. Years of wanting to run away or just die. Thinking, *Why would God give me what I ask for. I haven't given Him what He asked for. What His son had died for.*

So, like earlier, enter Cheryl. Watching how people would come up to her, total strangers, and pour out their life to her. How her faith carried her through. Watching her talk to people about their faith. Watching her be willing to pray before doing anything else. When we had a drive-thru nativity, she always signed up for the end booth. That's where they would ask the people who came through if they had any prayer requests. If they wanted prayer now and she would pray for them. Her prayers were always from the heart. I would say that if I could pick anyone to pray for me, she would be my first choice.

She would guide me through my walk by wanting to do Bible studies together. Work on church projects together. Encourage me to go be with the men and helping them in their walks. It took years to learn how because I would always pull from my past, not where God was leading me. Needless to say, I probably gave some wrong advice. Thankfully, I can see where the men would not listen to me then. Through God's grace, I was able to draw from the Holy Spirit, to give wiser advice. It's still hard to get men to understand how much the Holy Spirit is needed in their lives. How much their faith would grow if they would just trust in Jesus and the Holy Spirit.

One thing that I used to struggle with was when I prayed, was I praying to God or Jesus? If I would call on the Father, would Jesus still hear me? I would later fall on to the words of Jesus when they asked about seeing the Father. Jesus said in John 14:9: Whoever has seen me has seen the Father. So, I feel that if I pray to God, Jesus hears. If I pray to

Jesus, God hears. To whomever I pray, the Holy Spirit hears and sometimes helps me to say what needs to be said.

That's one thing that this journey has led me to. When I didn't think God was there. When I thought that He didn't hear my pleas. He was guiding me to where I am. He had a purpose for me and I believe that is where I am now. Telling people of God's love, mercy and grace. Leading them to Jesus and the Kingdom of God.

For a few years, we would try to get people inspired to come to a new Bible study. To a new class. To open their hearts up to the Spirit, but often, only a few would answer. Only a few would allow their life to be put on hold to learn more about what God had in store for them. We even tried golf outings to show people that you were not giving up your life, your hobbies, your fun, to follow God. That there's a lot of fun in following God. A joy that is truly beyond understanding. We still try to get people to see that.

Remembering my days when I was really involved in church. It seemed like it was only yesterday. My second wife and kids were getting really into church. We had moved back into the old neighborhood. We started attending my old church, the one that we had gotten married in. It wasn't long until I was elected Sunday School Superintendent. Opening and closing church. Our new pastor was involved in the lay ministry in our church organization, the Lutheran Church. I agreed to work in it. While in training, I was having Bible studies at our church during the week. A few of the old faithful would show up and it was good. I preached a couple times. Couldn't get anyone else in our congregation to work in the ministry but I sure had a lot of critics. Even through this, I was on an emotional high.

My downfall— it started to be all about me. What I thought was best for the church. How I wanted the congregation to get out and invite people into the church. They wouldn't be the disciples they were called to be. It was the preacher's job to bring people into the church. How they got it all wrong.

Some things never change. Years later, we still have the same problems. People will not commit and they expect others to do what they feel they are not qualified to do.

## Chapter Eighteen

I don't like to fly. I have always been fascinated by airplanes. Really, anything that flies. I have bought myself cheap birthday gifts. You know, those gifts you want and no one else has a clue what you want. I've done this for birthdays and Christmas. I have bought mostly small helicopters that I tried to learn how to fly. Learned how to crash.

I never flew until I went into the service. A flight from Roanoke, Virginia, to Nashville, Tennessee, by way of Atlanta, Georgia. Didn't make sense to me to have to go all the way down just to come back up. I would fly a few more times, until the last time. I flew halfway around the world. To a country called Vietnam.

The last time was when Cheryl talked me into flying to Colorado. We got sick on the day of the flight and had to postpone, but we would do it later. We left out of Tri-Cities Airport to Atlanta. After about a three-hour layover, we took off. Fifteen minutes into the flight, the captain said that he had never had to say this, but we had to turn around. We had to turn around and go back to the airport. Something was wrong with the plane. We exchanged planes and everything went fine. The second plane actually was worse looking than the first. No one ever told us what was wrong with that plane. I never flew again.

We have a couple friends who are pilots for major companies and airlines. Another friend who got his private pilot's license. These guys really do like to get up in the air. I still look up into the sky to watch the planes. The military jets practice low flying techniques. To see those new jets come over just a few hundred feet off the ground then zoom away is so fascinating. All the military craft flying over are fun to watch. The Ospreys, the helicopters, the big tankers practicing refueling procedures. It all takes my breath away. One time at work, we were mining on top of a hill and an F-16 flew by, lower than we were. I looked down to see the pilot. What a sight. I bet he wasn't a hundred feet off the ground.

We often get to see wonders that will always remain in our minds. The stories we get to tell about our life. Just like this one. There's a couple of stories that I tell to why I quit flying. The second one you have already read about, the other one, you are about to.

I was on my way to Spring Training one year. My son had asked me to fly. It would be quicker and cheaper. I had said okay. I flew out of Tri-Cities Airport in Blountville, Tennessee. It was March and, of course, it was windy. It was a small plane and with the wind, you could feel the turbulence. We flew from there to Nashville where I was to board my connecting flight. The wind was horrendous. As the plane was landing, we could feel and see the plane going sideways. It was scary. I thought, *Okay, the larger plane will be more stable.* Wrong. We could feel the air pushing us sideways as we were taking off and the ride was rough all the way. We landed in Orlando, Florida, and was I glad to be on the ground. I stayed with my son for a week and then headed back home.

I arrived at the airport and a gentleman checked my baggage outside. I thought that was convenient. Went into the terminal and checked in to make sure I was good. The clerk said okay and issued me my new ticket. Well, wouldn't you know, the destination was wrong. There apparently were two William Wagner's at that airport. One heading to Cincinnati, Ohio, and the other heading to Bristol, Tennessee. I go back to the desk and tell the attendant that this is wrong. She checked everything to verify, then called for my luggage to be brought to the desk. I forgot to tell you that before I found the mistake. I was selected at random for a body check. I had to empty all my pockets, take my shoes off, and then they waved me with that wand to see if I had anything on me.

So, after all that was done, I corrected their mistake and had to go to another terminal where my baggage was randomly selected to be x-rayed for illegal materials. That took another 30 minutes. Then I had to go through another screening because I had been randomly selected. After being so randomly selected, I finally got on another flight to Charlotte, North Carolina. It was a different airline. When I arrived in Charlotte, I had to proceed to another part of the terminal where I was randomly picked to be checked again. I felt that because of the original mistake they were watching me. I finally made it back to Bristol where I vowed that I would never fly again. But of course, I did, one more time.

I'm still fascinated with planes. I love to look at the streams they make in the sky. The roar of the engines fighting against the head winds. The sound of the helicopters flying over and always, the military jets.

## Chapter Nineteen

After all these escapades of flying, we decided to drive. Cheryl had taken up golf and had gotten pretty good at it in such a short time. We decided to drive when we went to Colorado and see what this country was like. There is so much beauty this country has to offer. The national monuments. The national parks. The off-the-beaten-path adventures that you can't find in a travel brochure.

We would often go to professional golf outings to see our favorite golfers. Those who were way better than we were. To just get another view of courses and meet different people. Maybe get lucky and get to see a professional golfer up close, which we did. It was at one of the outings in North Carolina that we met an interesting couple. I have forgotten their names, but they said that they had played golf in about every state in the southern 48. Wow. Now that would be a challenge. We also got to see some uses for old golf clubs and balls while we were chatting with them. So now we had a purpose other than just seeing the country.

I think to date, it has been 30 out of 48 that we have played in. Maybe a few more. I can't recall unless I go check our score cards. We started collecting scorecards and logo golf balls from every course that we played. Some really nice courses and some hole-in-the-wall courses. One we played in Arizona was renovated from an old, borrowed pit for the interstate highway. The carts had been turned on and the keys removed. You bought your round out of a vending machine, 9 or 18 holes. You could by tees, gloves, and snacks, out of that vending machine. It was just a 9-hole course but you could go it twice to get in 18. While playing that one, a very strong wind came up with some dark clouds. I thought we might get a tornado, but it was just dark clouds and wind. We played on. The wind was so strong, Chery's hair, which was in a ponytail, was blowing straight out. I couldn't keep my hat on. I tried hitting into the wind but my ball wouldn't go very far. It was getting darker, so we were deciding to quit, but as soon as it started, it stopped.

Those are just a couple of adventures we had playing different golf courses. Not your uptown, Trent Jones trail golf courses, but your mom-and-pop courses that are just fun to play. From 9-hole courses to 18-hole courses on the side of a mountain. From coal strip mining land that was transformed because someone had an idea. Courses where it said to beware of the alligators to watching eagles soar. We have played from the east coast to the west coast. From Texas to Maine. Minnesota to Louisiana. It has been a true joy. We once thought we would hike some of the Appalachian Trail, until we figured out how rough the ground was. There's nothing like a Holiday Inn king-size bed. We were in Maine on our honeymoon and we thought we would walk some of the trail there. We pulled into the state park there and we could see the mountain that was the end of the Appalachian Trail. Our thinking was that there was a parking area there and we would just park and walk up the mountain. Have our picture taken and that would be that. Didn't work that way. The ranger said it was a twenty-mile hike to the end of the Appalachian Trail from the parking area. Well, that ended that conquest. He was very nice and gave us a map and some brochures on the trail. There were a lot of restrictions on the trail that we hadn't planned on. Motto of the story? Don't try to skirt corners.

We did get to see a lot of natural wonders and go to the most eastern end of the United States. We made it to the West Quoddy Head Light in Lubec, Maine. The first and only lighthouse that we saw. We could also see Nova Scotia from there. It was beautiful, windy and cold. While looking for the entrance to the park, we also got to see our first moose. They are awesome animals. This guy was about nine feet tall and he waded out into the water until just his head was showing, so he could eat the grass that was floating in the water. On our trip through Maine, we also saw our first eagle's nest. It was in the middle of the interstate. It was huge. It had been built in between two light poles. That nest must have been at least 8-foot by 10-foot.

Those are some joys that you can't see from the air. Things that are off the beaten path. It's one thing to see them in a zoo, but to see them in their natural habitat, you can see God's handy work.

The love of golf has taken us places we only read about or seen on television. Places like the Atlantic Ocean, the Pacific Ocean, Mount Rushmore, The Grand Tetons, The Petrified Forest, Yellowstone National Park and its Hot Springs like Old Faithful, The Grand Canyon and the lands of the Arizona Indians, The beauty of the Mountains of Utah and the Great Salt Lake, Crossing the mighty Mississippi River several times and it always looks the same. Being from little old Southwest Virginia, not many people get to see these great wonders. We get a feel of how the pioneers felt when they set out for new land. Not knowing what to expect and not having the conveniences that we enjoy today. God created this land for us to enjoy and take care of. When you see the beauty that is there, you can understand what His plan is for us. We still have many wonders that we would like to see before we get too old.

## Chapter Twenty

What a journey it has been? There is so much in one's life that can't be put into words. The birth of your children. The divorce and heartache that you go through. The times you spent in a combat zone with new friends, not knowing what tomorrow will bring. Just trying to get through it. The struggles with your parents after adulthood. No one can see these through your eyes. We all remember these events differently.

There are events in my life that I can't remember. Things before the age of six. My oldest son only remembers age seven and after. He broke his right arm at age four, but he only recalls it at age seven.

I had this kid at age twelve who was always kind of shy. He was a good kid. I would pick him up to take him to football practice and sometimes take him home. I remember the practices and the smiles he had on his face. Years later, still in his teens, he killed someone. He got three life sentences. We contacted each other years later, and he was looking to get a new trial. I guess that is still in the works. He asked if I could write a letter to the court to help him get a new trial. I told him that I only remember the twelve-year-old kid. We communicated for a while, then I stopped. I have thought about that for a long time. I had told him that God probably forgave him for what he had done, but man will still make him pay for what he had done.

I think of all the places I have been and the things that I have done and wonder how I lived this long. In a combat zone. On a plane that an engine catches on fire. Turned away from a ride with a customer only to see that passenger side crushed later. One time, I threw a piece of metal up on to a platform only to have it come right back at me. I turned my face, fearing it would hit me in the head, only to hear the metal land several feet away. Going through two divorces where suicide is an ever-present possibility. Only to find that I can write.

Writing three books on how to draw closer to God through His word and the prompting of the Holy Spirit. Devotionals that I am in awe of and ones that I still post daily.

I pause and reflect on all that has happened to me. Sons that have wonderful lives. Daughters who have struggled with relationships. Grandchildren that make you so proud just in making good decisions. Are they all good decisions? Well, time will tell. They are all still young in their life. The best thing I can do for them is to show them what a wonderful God I serve. How He has blessed me in so many ways. That His purpose for me has led me to where I am. I am humbled by His mercy and grace. I will sing His praises all the days of my life. Will I do everything right? Not hardly. Will I fail you, my family, my friends? More than likely. But I know I serve an Almighty God who never fails. Who has a plan for me and that plan will never fail. I will cause it to struggle some, but in the end, it will all come around to His will for me.

# Epilogue

What will I take away from here? There are so many great Christian authors out there who will help you navigate this life. The walk with Christ will be very tough at times. Your questions will not always be answered. Your prayers will not always be answered. If you submit to the Father, you will know that it is His Will that will be done and not yours. You will see friends come and go. People who you loved and grew up with will forget your name. You will watch friends die way too young. Maybe you will have a sibling who will take their life, and you grasp for answers. You will lose your parents and then have no where to turn for guidance. You will then become the parent who has to have the answers. You never saw this coming. You never thought you would make it this far. You may have thought that you would never see fifty, much less 70. There has been one thing that has always been constant. God has always been with you. You look back and see how you had given your life early to Him, but you left Him outside. He stood outside the door knocking. Remember me? I called you by name. I let you have your time in the world, now it is My time with you. Follow Me. Embrace the Holy Spirit. Let's see where this will lead and who we can take with us.